Some Bygone Scenes of Brixton and Its People

Arthur L. Clamp

Maypole Dancers in 1930
These were the school girls of the village and displayed their skills at the annual Sports Day and Flower Show held in the gardens of Elbridge House. The Yealmpton Brass Band was always in attendance.

This version of the book is virtually as originally published.
There are now additional pages at the back providing information about the author.

The republishing project is being managed by Arthur's grandson, Steven Gibson. We aim to find all the research that he was involved in publishing, preserving it for the next generation as part of 'The Clamp Collection'.

Introduction

THIS illustrated booklet records many aspects of the life of Brixton village which have now largely gone although at the time it was probably thought that these were features that would last for many years. As is so often the case, changes take place very quickly and scenes and events alter almost without anyone thinking much about them.

Brixton is the first true country village on the main A379 road linking Plymouth with the South Hams. Numerous developments have taken place on the eastern side of Plymouth but to date these have not infringed upon its locality.

Since the earlier account of the parish given on page 4, Brixton has attracted families who have had quite large residences built in the village such as Elbridge House, Brixton House, etc. and their occupants have often taking a leading role in village life by opening their houses and gardens for various events and contributing to the prosperity of the area. Notable among these have been the Moon family, Penryce Lyons family and the Scott family. There are others, of course, who were linked to the village school, farms, businesses and the church and chapel.

A stepping stone in the changing way of life in this area was the opening of the branch railway line from Friary Station in Plymouth to Yealmpton in 1898. Brixton Road station and Steer Point halt enabled people and goods to reach Plymouth markets and other places more quickly and also enabled some people to live in the village and work in Plymouth. Carriers from various places in the South Hams were until then the only means of getting about and these were normally scheduled once or twice a week. Perhaps the closing of the line in 1947 to passengers is now a matter of regret as the unforeseen increases in road traffic, bringing now almost intolerable conditions in the village, would have offset this increase by people using the line instead of their car.

However, for most men up until the Second World War employment was either on the land, in the brickworks at Steer Point or the vineries at Elburton. A few men worked in Devonport Dockyard but this required a daily walk down to Laira Bridge to catch a boat. The fact that many men worked in these areas gave rise to quite a well integrated village society with almost all people knowing one another and most joining in one activity or another as shown by the photographs in this booklet.

The last war affected Brixton to a greater extent than one would at first think. The locality was designated as a zone for attracting enemy planes away from Plymouth by starting various large fires and the local homeguard discharged their responsibilities admirably by assisting and training from their hut at Brixton Road garage. There were no direct attacks on the village but many explosives fell roundabout doing minor damage.

The past few decades have brought about many changes in the way of building new council and private houses and recently a new school and excellent community centre. People have come here to retire from London and Venn Court has enabled these and local persons, to enjoy their years of retirement in very pleasant surroundings.

Shops and businesses now tend to change hands more often than was the case but the butchers are still run by the Clarke family, the petrol station has closed and some farm buildings have been converted into dwellings.

Changes are, of course, inevitable and in many instances these are for the better. This record of Brixton village life should capture some of the passing changes and bring back memories of ways of life that are now gone. The advent of television, and now satellite TV viewing will likely make more inroads into the amount of time people will put to village events but it is hoped that through local organisations, such as the British legion, Brixton will still maintain a distinctive village way of life.

Acknowledgements

The preparation of this booklet was greatly assisted with the help of many people and I wish to thank them for their time and enthusiasm in getting this record of their village life into print. First I must thank Mr. Ken West whose persistence in getting me started has at last been rewarded. Other people have kindly loaned photographs and supplied information and made suggestions about other aspects of Brixton which have yet to be followed up.

These are Mrs. S. Furzeland, Mr. Bob Mashford, Mrs. K. Tregidgo, Mrs. E. Tanner, Mr. and Mrs. Elford James, Mrs. Elizabeth O'Neill, Mrs. M. Cardew, Mrs. D. Arnold, Mr. G. Taylor, Mrs. F. Scott, Mrs. P. Sharpe and Snawdons, Ltd., Yealmbridge.

I have omitted to include the farming life of the parish as there is sufficient information to make up another title to complement this one on the village.

Arthur Clamp
203 Elburton Road,
Plymouth, Devon PL9 8HX

Brixton School and Park

A very early photograph probably taken in the 1890s showing two elm trees remaining from a line of them planted in 1677 by Mr. Fortescue of Spriddlestone as a source of income for the poor when they were cut and sold as timber. These two remaining trees were felled later and then cut into timber for building purposes. Note the Victorian dress worn by the children.

St. Mary's Church 1907

The lamp standard is in its original position on the village green and Church Cottages were then thatched like many other houses. The James family lived in them for many years. It would be interesting to know the names of the children posing for the visiting photographer and those standing by the door.

Before the Road Widening

The cottage on the left, once the home of Charlie James and his family, was demolished in 1963. This late 1940s photo will bring back many memories of this sharp corner.

Brixton Parish

This extract comes from the 1822 edition of Lyson's *Britannia Magna* and now makes interesting reading.

Charles Goad at the Post Office

This very early photo shows Mrs. Eliza James being held as a young baby at about the turn of the century. The former buildings on the site of the present post office, built 1910, are here with the shop window displaying a variety of sweets of now Edwardian vintage. Was the lady in the middle Mrs. Goad?

An Early Brixton Family

Proudly posing for the camera in their best clothes are Mr. and Mrs. Martin Rowse and their daughter, Violet, who lived at Elliott's Hill.

BRIXTON, anciently BRITRICHESTON, in the hundred and deanery of Plympton, lies about two miles from Plympton, and four from Plymouth.

The manor belonged anciently to a family which took its name from the place. The husband of the elder co-heiress of William de Britricheston, who died in the reign of Henry III., took the name of Britricheston; and his posterity continued to possess this manor for seven generations. Vincent Calmady, Esq., purchased it of the representatives of this family about the middle of the sixteenth century, and fixed his residence here; his descendant, Sir Shilston Calmady, was succeeded in the possession of this estate, in the reign of Charles I., by George Keinsham. It was sold by the latter, in 1652, to Sampson Sandys, of whose descendant it was purchased in 1717 by Thomas Veale, Esq. of Coffleet in this parish. It is now, together with Coffleet, the property of the Rev. Richard Lane, whose father was nephew of Mr. Veale.

Brixton English belonged anciently to the family of English, and afterwards successively to the Blomvilles and Coplestons of Bowdon. It was purchased, after the decease of Thomas Copleston, Esq., in 1758, by Mr. Veale, and is now the property of the Rev. Richard Lane.

Brixton Reigny belonged to the family of Reigny, whose co-heiresses married Crabb, Prous, and Horcy. It was afterwards in the Heles of Wollaton, and was bequeathed, in 1635, by Elizæus Hele, to charitable uses.

Spridleston belonged, in the reign of Henry III., to William Spriddle, whose family possessed it for six generations; it was afterwards in the Fortescues; and became, in the reign of Henry VI., the seat of John, third son of John Fortescue, Esq., of Wimpston; with the heiress of this branch it passed to the Fortescues of Buckland Filleigh. The late Richard Inglett, Esq., (who inherited Spridlestone, and took the name of Fortescue,) sold this estate, in 1785, to Mr. Lane, of Coffleet, and it is now the property of his son. The old mansion of the Fortescues is inhabited by a farmer.

Harston, at an early period, was successively in the families of Reynald, Harston, and Silverlock; afterwards in the Carslakes, whose heiress brought it to Wood. The Woods resided here for several generations; it is now the property of their representative, John Wood Winter, Esq., who resides at Lower Harston; the old mansion of the Woods, built in the reign of Henry VII., was in part destroyed by an accidental fire, in the beginning of the last century; the remaining part, including the hall and chapel, is inhabited by a farmer.

Sherford was the ancient inheritance of the Maynards: it belonged afterwards to the Drakes of Buckland Monachorum, and having passed with that estate, is now the property of Thomas Trayton Fuller Elliott Drake, Esq.

Wollaton was a seat of the Heles, and so continued till the death of Elizæus Hele in 1635: it passed afterwards to the Pollexfens, and is now the property of their descendant, Edmund Pollexfen Bastard, Esq. M. P. Mr. Bastard possesses also the manor of Halwell in this parish, which belonged, at an early period, for eight generations, to the family of Britt. The heiress of Britt brought it to the Wises. In 1667 it was sold by Sir Edward Wise to Sir William Morice; one of the co-heiresses of Sir Nicholas Morice brought it to Sir John Molesworth, Bart., of whose descendant, Sir William Molesworth, Bart., it was purchased about 1789 by the late Mr. Bastard.

In the parish church, (which is a daughter-church to Plympton[o],) are memorials of the families of Wood[o] and Lane[p], and the tomb of Walter Hele, father of Elizæus Hele, the inscription on which is obliterated: he died about the year 1613.

The tithes of Brixton were appropriated to the monastery of Plympton, afterwards to the dean and chapter of Windsor: in 1800 they were sold under the powers of the land-tax redemption act to Thomas Splatt, Esq., the present proprietor. The dean and chapter are still patrons of the perpetual curacy. Elizæus Hele, before mentioned, bequeathed the sum of 415*l*. for a preaching minister at Brixton; this sum was laid out in the purchase of lands in the parish of Modbury, which now produce 33*l*. 11*s*. 8*d*. per annum. The benefice has been augmented by a parliamentary grant, and the perpetual curate has 20*l*. per annum out of the tithes. John Quick, an eminent non-conformist divine, author of a History of the Reformation in France, and other works, was ejected from the living of Brixton in 1662.

Near the church-yard is a fine grove of elms planted in the year 1677 by Mr. Fortescue, of Spridlestone, and other parishioners, for the expressed purpose of being sold, when at a proper growth, to raise a fund for the benefit of the poor, as appears by an inscribed stone[q]: a singular instance of prudent foresight, and well worthy of imitation, there being many parishes in which small wastes might most beneficially be thus planted.

Church Annual Outing in 1946

Probably going to Goodrington seen here with Mrs Violet Reade looking from her window. Recognised are Mrs. Furzeland, Miss Ottley, Mr. and Mrs. S. Dannon, Mrs. W. Clarke, Mrs. E. Furzeland, Mrs. E. Pengelley, Mrs. M. Lovegrove, Mrs. D. Davis, Miss Valerie Davis, Mrs. A. Betts, Mrs. S. Davis, Mrs. F. Revell, W. Buckingham, Mauria Light, Valerie Davis, Mrs. E. Chaffe, Mrs. M. Yeoman and Mrs. Barnes.

Buckets and Spades Ready for the Beach 1947/48

A Sunday School outing about to leave Brixton with Pat James, Linda James, Lorraine Ffoukes, Jeffery Ffoukes, Bunty Mann, David Wilmington, Mrs. A. Ffoukes, Mrs. Yabsley, Peggy Gully, Amy James, Mrs. Eva Sprague, Mrs. Vera James, Christine Wilmington, Phillamina Sprague, Bertha James, Mrs. Violet Ames, Mrs. B. Gully, Mrs. E. James, Mrs. W. Sprague, Mrs. L. Pethick, Mrs. W. Avery, Mr. MartinRowse, Elisabeth Gosling, Mrs. W. Mann and Mrs. E. Oxland.

Old Brixtonians
Bill Taylor and his wife Harriett are outside their cottage near the pump. A very early photo. Bill worked as a roadman and they had two children Sidney and Seymour.

Brixton Park
Appropriately called Park House and Park Cottage the two top houses were once the home of Joseph Cawse and family and Alfred Yabsley and family. The right hand building was once used as a slaughterhouse and butchery. Mr. & Mrs. Ernie Taylor also undertook contract work from here using his horse and cart at another date.

Brixton A.F.C. Team, 1930s
They played in the Churches League and had their pitch near Cofflete Lodge. Recognised are Alf Budge, Mr. Tom James, George Jackson, Jack Mumford, Bill Lillicrap, Frank Mumford, Sid Gully, Albert Davis and Mr. Bishop.

Y.M.C.A. Football Team
Members are assembled on the village green among whom are D. Ryder, G. Sprague, C. Sprague, T. Bates, D. Hodges, I. Langford, K. Clegg, R. Goldsmith with others under the leadership of Derek O'Neill.

Teacher goes to School in 1937
£28.00 cleared this Excelsior motorbike of purchase price and tax paid for by the mother of Miss Millicent Jackson who then taught at South Milton school. She made the twice daily journey from Brixton Torr stopping at Walter's garage at Modbury for fuel where a can had been set aside for her use.

Under Instructions
Dereck O'Neill is offering advice here to members of the football team linked to the village Y.M.C.A. Graham Sprague has been recognised here sometime in the 1950s.

Miss Hilda Drake's Class 1926

She is well remembered not only for her long service at Brixton School but for her daily cycle ride from her home at Wembury to the school! Seen here are Harry Smallridge, Henry Hosegood (son of the headmaster), Harry Radmore, Roy Steer, Oswald Mumford, Rosie Medland, Queenie Rowse, Sylvia Davis, Alan James and others. Note that some of the children are kneeling on rubber mats in the first row.

Brixton and Elburton Children in the early 1930s

No teacher is with this group posed in the school yard or play ground. The occasion cannot be recalled but names can. These are Douglas James, Archie Radmore, Rodney Gosling, Doreen Yabsley, Marian Davis, Martha Radmore, Florie Taylor and Fred Wilmington. Others have already been named in different groups. Some Elburton children preferred this school to that at Plymstock which was about the same walking distance.

Manor House and Cottages

Charles Goad was the sub-postmaster when this view was taken about 1918. He also ran the grocery shop next door and the two thatched cottages, now renovated, were the homes of Mrs. Greep and Mr. and Mrs. Gully.

Foxhound Inn 1900-1910

This very early view was taken when Richard Chaffe was its licensee. The gas lamp and clothes worn by the two girls show another part of the local scene. The trees, of course, have gone but the Manor House is yet to be built by Mr. James Moon in 1910 further down the road.

Brixton Children

The occasion cannot be recalled but it is thought to be at Mudbank or Steer Point. The period is just pre-First World War. The dresses indicate a special event of some kind.

Winstone Hamlet

The cottages on the left of the unmade road running down to Mudbank housed workers on the Kitley Estate and the large right hand cottage was the home of the estate's game-keeper William Harris for many years. The view comes from the 1920s.

Fordbrook Farm

Mrs. Mary West, wife of Albert West then farming here, stands at the rear of the farm against the large kitchen where the two chimneys indicate the position of the range and the copper boiler to the right. Further to the right was where the cider pound or press stood.

Brixton Vicarage

This was built in 1904 on land given by Mr. Bastard. It was the home of Rev. Charles E. Green until 1910 then the Rev. Frederick W. Hewitt succeeded to the living. The house stands alone, not surrounded by trees and houses as it does nowadays.

Elliott's Hill
Poll Elliott had the shop marked *Harris* here for many years while John Husk ran the family newsagents business just below it. This 1940s photo brings to mind this familiar part of the village.

The Wheelwright's Shop
A once familiar activity in many villages when various farm carts, wheels and implements were repaired. The two men have not been identified but one is probably James Mann who ran this business for about twenty-five years until his son took over in the early 1930s.

A Group of Locals
Richard Chaffe was probably the licensee here when this very view was recorded. The house in the background, once the home of Russell Furzeland and his family, was later demolished. The date of this scene and the men in it are not known.

On Arrival at Paignton

This was one of the more popular destinations for a day's outing for Brixton families. The crowded open char-a-banc indicates its popularity. No doubt many families will be recognised here and the ladies dresses confirms that it was sometime in the 1920s.

Brixton in about 1905

This postcard is franked 1908 and shows local children and a few adults by the green. Note the thatched building and the building on the left demolished in 1963 for road widening. The James family lived in it for many years.

Open Top and Hard Tyres

Another of the once popular char-a-banc outings seen here away from Brixton carrying members of the Radmore, West, Yabsley and Smallridge families. It is in the 1920s and *Rex Tours* ran from a Plymouth office.

PROGRAMME.

President :—Commander A. Penrice-Lyons, D.S.O., R.N.
Chairman—F. Crocker, Esq.

Grounds Open at 2 p.m.   Tea from 4.   Sports at 2-30.
Presentation of Flower Show Prizes at 8 p.m.
Dancing on the Green from 7-30 to 9.
The TORPOINT TOWN BAND will be in attendance

Sports Programme.

Commencing at 2-30.

JUNIORS.
1. Flat Race, boys 4 and 5
2. Flat Race, boys 6
3. Flat Race, boys 7
4. Flat Race, girls 4 and 5
5. Flat Race, girls 6 and 7
6. Flat Race, girls and boys 4 and 5
7. Flat Race, girls 8 and 9
8. Flat Race, boys 8 and 9
9. Wheelbarrow Race, boys 8 and 9
10. Three-legged Race, girls 8 and 9

SENIORS.
1. 80 yards sprint, under 12
2. 100 yards, 12 and over, boys or girls
3. High Jump, 2 per team
4. Three-legged Race, boys or girls
5. Team Race, Teams of 4
6. Sack Race, boys
7. Skipping Race, girls
8. Obstacle Race

Events 7 to 10 in the Junior Section and all Senior Events count for points in the Competition for the School Sport's Cup, Presented by Commander Penrice-Lyons.

LOCAL EVENTS AT 5-30.

		PRIZES VALUE OF				PRIZES VALUE OF		
1	100 yards	5/-	3/-	2/-	6 One Mile	10/-	7/6 5/-	2/6
2	Ladies' Race, (Married)	5/-	3/-	2/-	7 Veterans' Race (Men over 40— one yard for each year	5/-	3/-	2/-
3	Quarter-Mile	5/-	3/-	2/-				
4	Ladies' Race, (Single)	5/-	3/-	2/-	8 Obstacle Race	5/-	3/-	2/-
5	High Jump	5/-	3/-	2/-				

Horticultural Schedule.

JUDGES :—Messrs. D. CALTHORPE and GUNNINGHAM.

LOCAL CLASSES.—Entrance Fee 3d. each Class.

Class		1st	2nd	3rd
1	Six Round Potatoes	3 0	2 0	1 0
2	Six Kidney Potatoes	3 0	2 0	1 0
3	Five Heavy Weight Potatoes any variety (cleaned)	3 0	2 0	1 0
4	Two Cabbages	3 0	2 0	1 0
5	Six Autumn-sown Onions	3 0	2 0	1 0
6	Six Spring-sown Onions	3 0	2 0	1 0
7	Twelve Runner Beans	3 0	2 0	1 0
8	Twelve Broad Beans	3 0	2 0	1 0
9	Six Carrots	3 0	2 0	1 0
10	Six Parsnips	3 0	2 0	1 0
11	Three Beet (Globe)	3 0	2 0	1 0
12	Three Turnips	3 0	2 0	1 0
13	Six Leeks	3 0	2 0	1 0
14	Twelve Eschalots	3 0	2 0	1 0
15	Twenty Pods of Green Peas	3 0	2 0	1 0
16	Three Lettuces	3 0	2 0	1 0
17	Six Cooking Apples	3 0	2 0	1 0
18	Six Dessert Apples	3 0	2 0	1 0
19	Dish of Gooseberries	3 0	2 0	1 0
20	Dish of Currants	3 0	2 0	1 0
21	Two Ridge Cucumbers	3 0	2 0	1 0
22	Two Marrows	3 0	2 0	1 0
23	Heaviest Weight Marrow	3 0	2 0	1 0
24	Collection of Vegetables, 6 kinds, for Amateurs	8 0	5 0	3 0
25	Twelve Sprays of Parsley	3 0	2 0	1 0
26	Three Sticks of Rhubarb	3 0	2 0	1 0

FLOWERS.

		1st	2nd	3rd
1	Collection of Asters	2 6	1 6	1 0
2	Collection of Dahlias	2 6	1 6	1 0
3	Six Vases of Sweet Peas, 6 varieties	2 6	1 6	1 0
4	Best Collection of Gladioli	2 6	1 6	1 0
5	Best Bunch of Garden Flowers	2 6	1 6	1 0
6	Best Collection of Carnations	2 6	1 6	1 0

First Prize in Class 6 given by Mr. E. Yabsley, Steer Point.

Living Whist

This unusual form of playing this card game with children on the Elbridge lawn tennis court at the annual Brixton Flower Show and Sports Day can be seen here. Held on the last Saturday of July in the 1930s by permission of Mr. and Mrs. A. Penrice-Lyons, four players sit in the corners of the court. The joker then takes a child holding a card to the centre. The tricks are taken to one side and the winner moves around the area followed by all the children.

Old and Young
John Sharpe, here with a grandchild, was then the oldest resident in the village, well remembered with his smart white beard and, for this occasion in the 1940's, wearing a bowler hat.

Rev. F. Hewitt's Horse
Seen here probably between 1912 and 1914 being held by Owen Sharp the groom. The small wooden stable was in the grounds of the old vicarage. The Rev. Frederick W. Hewitt was killed attending wounded soldiers in France in September, 1915.

Brixton Y.M.C.A. 1932
At work on the new corrugated hut are Dave Gunney, Sid Yabsley, Elford James, Bill Yeoman, Albert Davis and Bert Stevens watched by Mr. Hosegood, headmaster and the Rev. Harry Vodden.

Brixton Home Guard about 1945

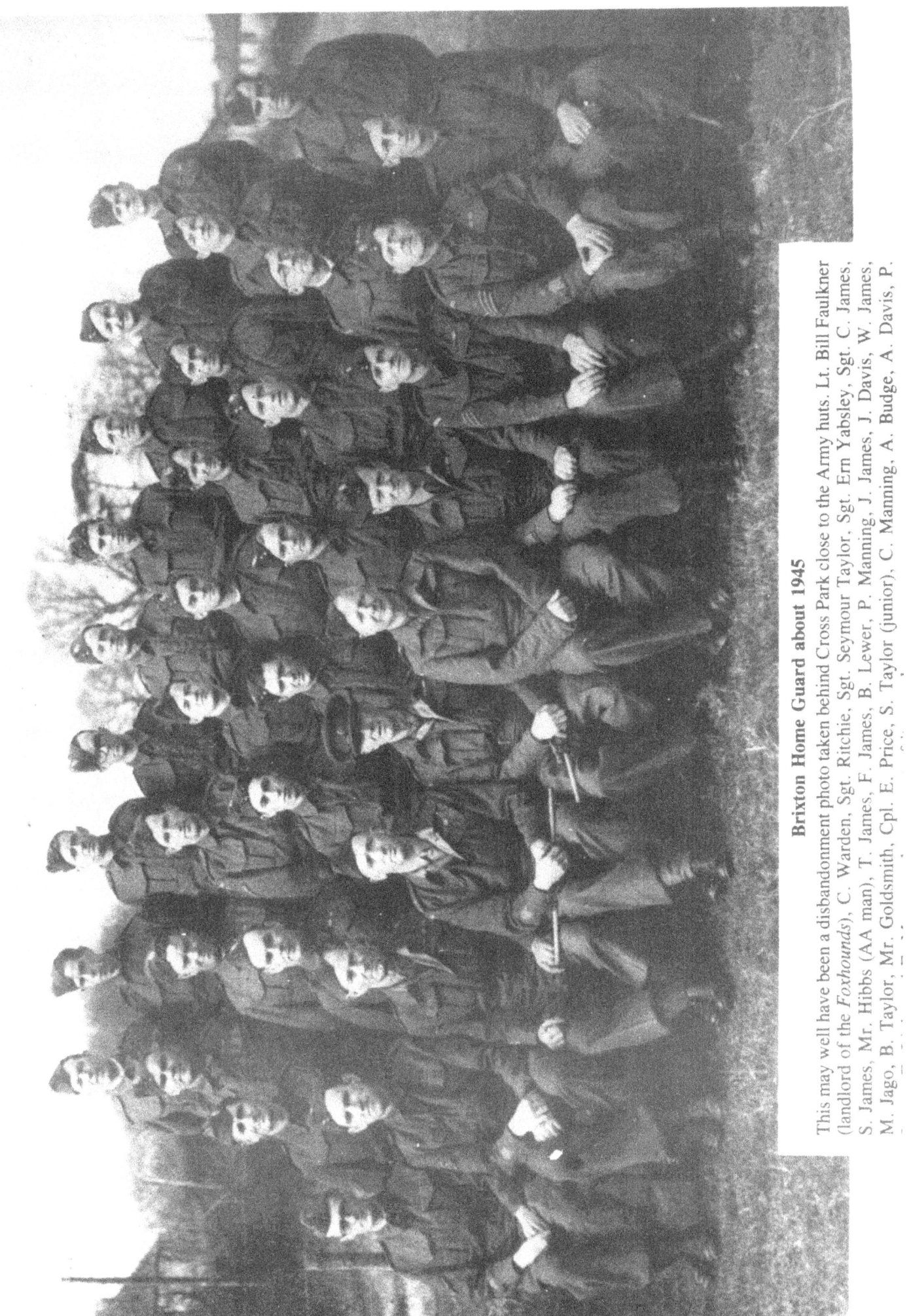

This may well have been a disbandonment photo taken behind Cross Park close to the Army huts. Lt. Bill Faulkner (landlord of the *Foxhounds*), C. Warden, Sgt. Ritchie, Sgt. Seymour Taylor, Sgt. Ern Yabsley, Sgt. C. James, S. James, Mr. Hibbs (AA man), T. James, F. James, B. Lewer, P. Manning, J. James, J. Davis, W. James, M. Jago, B. Taylor, Mr. Goldsmith, Cpl. E. Price, S. Taylor (junior), C. Manning, A. Budge, A. Davis, P.

Folk Dancing Group in 1985

Seen here under the direction of Mrs. Mavis Clooke are school pupils at the Church Garden Party at Elbridge House. They are Christopher Roberts, Richard Foulkes, James Kingdom, Miles Lockwood, David Powell, Daniel James, David Axell, Lisa Broom, Louise Horne, Lucy Skentelbury, Diane Parker, Jane Easterbrook, Irene and Theresa Godward, Alan Landricombe and Julie Evans.

1954 St. Mary's Church Garden Party

This has now been held in the grounds of Elbridge House for many years. Here Mr. and Mrs. Frank Scott with their daughter Jenny, are on the left, Mrs. Humphrey Woollcombe is in the centre and the Rev. Francis G. Powell, who was at Brixton from 1937 to 1960, is making the opening speech.

Fishing for Bottles

Mrs. Pat Ward is at one of the many stalls at Elbridge House carefully watching the attempts of Kirsty Goldsmith, Ray and Wendy Lee at retrieving bottled drinks, etc. while two children look on.

Local Men Working in Vinery Lane, Elburton

The horticultural trade provided employment for many Brixton men. Seen here are C. Wilmington, T. Gosling, H. Doddridge, L. John, H. Yabsley, J. West, W. Husk, M. Bennett, A. West, J. Birch, S. Davis, T. Bolt, C. Bidgood, W. Horswell and many others. This area of work was one of the main occupations for Brixton and Elburton people. It is in the 1930s.

Wartime Auxiliary Fire Service

The unit had a garage and rest room at Brixton Road garage which was opened in 1943 and disbanded in March, 1948. They had a car and light pump; four men were on duty each night, members taking it in turns to do this shift. Here can be seen Wallace West, Edgar James, Alf Thorne, John James, John Sherrell, Cyril Bidgood, Harold Luscombe, Frances Lawson, Wally Buckingham, Jim Williams, Jim West and others in front of their pump.

Methodist Church Fete
Then held in the grounds of Brixton House by permission of Mr. J. McBean in the 1950s, Ronald James stands with his grandson, Arthur, with other children enjoying the donkey cart ride.

A Day to Remember
Another late 1950's chapel annual fete held in June for many years before going to *Rosemont* where Mr. Heale then lived. Mr. Rowe and his daughter, Bertha, are in this scene at Brixton House gardens.

Brixton Chapel People
Adults and children pose in the grounds of the original chapel building showing Mr. D. Taylor, Mr. White, Mr. Blake, Mr. C. Blake, Mrs. I. White, Mrs. Dannen, Mrs. Eddy, Mr. Eddy, Mr. Congdon, Miss A. Horswill, Mrs. E. Hollywood, Mrs. Congdon, Mrs. E. West, Mrs. E. West, June Congdon, Muriel White, Majorie Pope, June Pope, Albert Pope, Shirley and Mervyn Congdon.

Practical School Lessons on the Land

Under the watchful eye of Mr. Albert Axworthy, headmaster, this 1914 photo shows the village children getting instruction on hoeing, raking and developing good gardening practices. Jim West and Cecil Harvey are here among boys striving to win the annual award given for the best plot. This was the old school gardens which later became allotments.

First British Legion Annual Dinner 1947

The hut was opened in 1946 and in November, 1947, the first of the annual dinners took place there. The president was Mr. Hutchings, chairman Jack Shoebridge, assistant secretary Miss Audrey Avery. Others here are Mr. and Mrs. E. James, Mr. and Mrs. Sid Gully, Mr. and Mrs. W. Barnes, Mr. Dusty James, Mr. & Mrs. E. Clarke, Mr. and Mrs. E. Price, Miss Ottley, Mr. and Mrs. A. Painter among many other local people.

Rabbiting at Spriddlestone

This once familiar activity is captured in this scene of 1949 when Les West, Ken West, E. Newcombe and Harold (Clickie) West and one other person assembled with two dogs, one called Spot, two guns and a line of seven rabbits. This was once a very popular pursuit and a source of food!

Brixton Torr Mills

This was the corn mill of old Cofflete House comprising of three floors of thirteen rooms. During the 1920s, 1930s and 1940s it was occupied by Jack Smallridge, Bertha and Edgar James, Freddie and Evelyn Chaffe, Harold and Gertrude West and F. Lear families until it was demolished in the 1950s.

Church Summer Fete, late 1940s

Mrs. Sprague organised the maypole dancing for this annual event which took place in the garden of Elbridge House in June. Dorothy James, Marjorie James, Margaret Painter, Joy James, Hilda Westcott, Betty Westcott, Suzanne Benbow and Valerie James are part of the dancing team watched by many local people on this occasion.

Albert James (Pickles)

Seen here delivering meat to Brixton from Tom Body's shop in Elburton. Cofflete lodge is on the left and this is the main road sometime in the early 1930s. Note the flowers in his jacket lapel and the telephone no. *Plymstock 3* on the bike plate!

Milk Delivery in the Village

Although milk and cream could be bought directly from the farms deliveries were undertaken from 1934 to 1940 by Mr. Radmore from Spriddlestone. He is seen here descending Red Lion Hill with Billy Radmore and, in the background, a small cart is also being carefully handled with, it is thought, produce from the then nearby allotments.

Elbridge House

This very fine house was built in the 1830s on land owned by the Rev. Richard Lane and it is recorded being occupied in 1839 by Penelope Lane; in 1850 by Captain Edmond Yonge (R.N.), 1878 by Mrs. Jane Yonge, 1897 by James Edward Yonge. From 1954 by Mrs. F. Scott and the late Mr. Scott who kindly allowed many garden parties to take place in the grounds and occasionally in the large house.

J. H. OTTLEY,
BRIXTON, Near Plymouth,
Tobacconist,
Groceries, Haberdashery, Household Requirements,
MINERALS AND ICES.

Wright's Cottage about 1912
Ten village children are suitably dressed for what was probably a special occasion with two boys playing by the 1897 lamp standard and others passing the shop once run by Miss Georgina K. Ottley and before by her parents Mr. and Mrs. John H. Ottley. It is now the *Sentry Box*.

1939: A Young Visitor to Brixton
The steps to the old school are on the right and in the far distance is the cottage Mr. and Mrs. James once occupied.

Old Brixton Family
This pre-1900 studio posed photo is of Gran and Granfer Samuel Davis. He came to Brixton to work on the building of the Yealmpton railway line and settled here having a large family.

New Houses in 1935
The first of six new houses built for the village at Cross Park by Martin Rowse and Harold James who were in partnership as builders. Also here are Bill Davis, Elford James, Sid Mumford; these were the first new houses to be built in the village.

Brixton Village A.F.C. in the late 1930s

The occasion for this group gathering cannot be recalled but some local boys are recognised with others from away. These are Norman Bennet, Owen Sharp, Jack Davis, Ern Pengelley, Ronald James, Cyril Bidgood and Wilf Husk. No doubt readers will recognise others here on the old football pitch upon which matches in the United Churches League regularly took place.

Brixton Village A.F.C. about 1912

This earliest photo of the football teams shows Rev. F. W. Hewitt, Bill Farleigh, Trace Mumford, Charlie Gully, W. Medland, Mr. Axworthy, headmaster, Martin Rowse, Arthur Annis, Rufus Sharp, Seymour Taylor, Bill James, Alfie Yabsley, Sid Yabsley, Bill Collier and Harold James, captain. They played on a field near Wollaton.

Bell Ringers after Practise
The *Sally* is being held here in this late 1930's group by St. Mary's Church with the old laundry house to Brixton House in the background. Recognised are Allen James, Frank James, Owen Sharp and Alf Venton.

Bellringing Contest at Bickleigh
Here Owen Sharpe, Frank James, Alf Venton, Elford James, captain, Alan James, William Davis proudly smile at their achievement in the late 1940s.

Winners of the Shield
This early 1950s group proudly displays Brixton's success in a bell ringing contest. The Rev. Frances G. Powell (1937 to 1960) stands with Sid Gully, Alf Venton, Owen Sharp, Frank James, Bill Davis and Allen James outside of St. Mary's Church.

Inter School Sports Challenge Shield 1930

Brixton often won this coveted shield given by Mr. Penrice-Lyons who was then a manager of the school. Millicent Jackson was the captain of the sports team made up of Douglas James, Sid Gully, Rosie Medland, Marian Davis, Kathleen Pengelley, Beryl Jackson, Sid Mumford, Fred Doddridge, Arthur Broad, Marian Macey and others.

St. Mary's Church Choir

In readiness for service at Brixton Church is Mrs. M. I. Gosling, Mrs. Andrews, Betty Bowering, Alice Davis, Ruth Davis, Mrs. Hammett Mr. C. McCarthy, Ann Ward, Alan Clegg, ? Small, ? Horswell, Clive Edmunds, Barbara Buttery, Ann Andrews, ? Small, David Bates with the Rev. Frances G. Powell and the organist Mr. Muttran. It is in the 1950s.

Mr. James and Grandson
One of the many old timers of the village who was a roadman seen here probably in the late 1920s in Old Road. Douglas, the grandson, was later to be taken prisoner of war at the Dunkirk evacuation in 1940.

Mothers' Union at Brixton
This was once a very flourishing group at St. Mary's Church. The photo dates from the 1930s and shows Mrs. R. Sharp, Mrs. E. Chaffe, Mrs. O. James with others carrying their banner outside St. Marys.

Brixton School Children 1929-30
These include Edward Gosling, Ken West, Stewart Avery, Gwen Doddridge, Olive James, Diane Chaffe, Sylvia Davis, Joan Macey, Fred Yabsley, Alan James, Joyce Light, Phyllis Head, Margaret Gosling, Catherine Yabsley, Oswald Mumford, Harry Smallridge, Fred Abel with Miss Hilda Drake their school mistress.

Brickworks Chimneys
Once a familiar sight for many miles around Steer Point they went together with the nearby building when the brickworks were modernised in the late 1960s.

Brickworks Quarrymen
This 1930s photo shows Sam Taylor, Harold West, Wallace West, Edgar James and ? Horton. They have quarried stone and clay which is taken by truck to be broken into small pieces ready for processing into bricks by the Western Counties Brick Company at Steer Point.

Railway Construction Workers

The branch line from Friary, Plymouth to Yealmpton opened on 15th January, 1898, and employed many local men in its construction. This group of eight workers looked dressed with ties which may well have been on the occasion of the opening of the line.

Steer Point Halt in 1928

Passengers alighted here for the ferry service to Newton Ferrers. Being near the brickworks, bricks were carried from here together with farm goods, some coal for local houses and oysters from the estuary beds. The line closed to passengers in 1930 but was reopened during the 1939-45 war only to close again for passengers in October, 1947. The rails were taken up in 1962.

Elburton Vineries Football Team

Made up mostly with Brixton men, the team played in the United Churches League. Seen here are Jim Coleman, Bill Davis, Fred Betts, Richard Annis, Percy Medland, Victor James, Albert James, Jim West, Horace Yabsley and two others. The year is in the late 1930s.

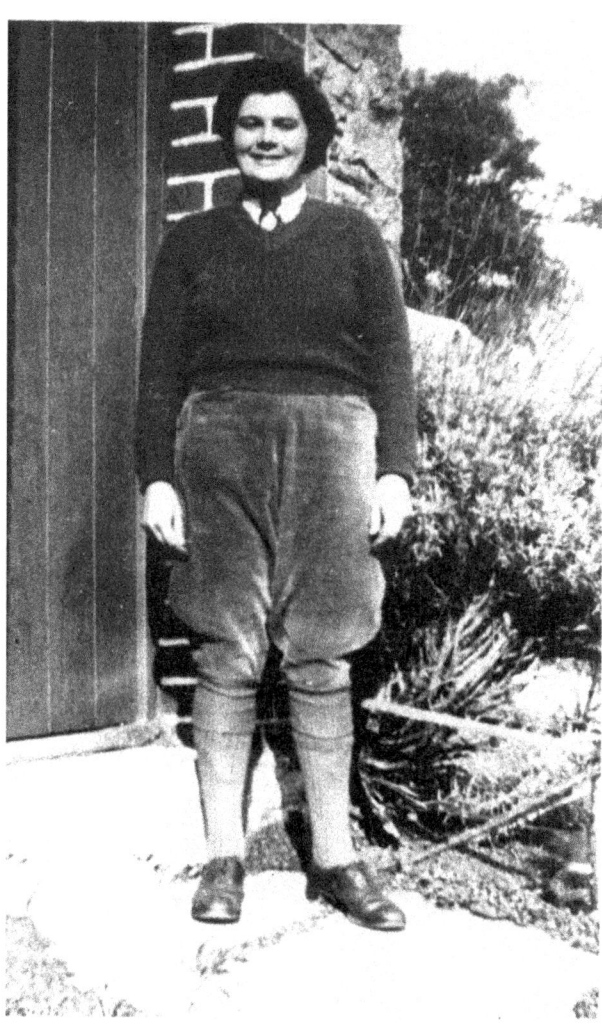

Land Army Girl
Queenie Rowse is here in her uniform in December, 1943, at Brixton Torr, one of many local girls who shared in the war effort by helping on the land. She is now Mrs. Yea.

An Outing to Brixton Torr
This has been a favourite place for many years to spend a Bank holiday at as shown by this group sitting on the tree trunk. Harold West, Gertrude West, Albert West with Joan Newcombe and daughter Maureen make up some of the members here in about 1950.

School Sports
Sometime between 1925-26 the school sports annual day involved George Sharpe, Iris Able, Queenie Rowse and Jack Hosegood seen here enjoying themselves.

Sports Certificate of 1930
This beautiful ornate certificate was presented to Millicent Jackson for her school record in the high jump.

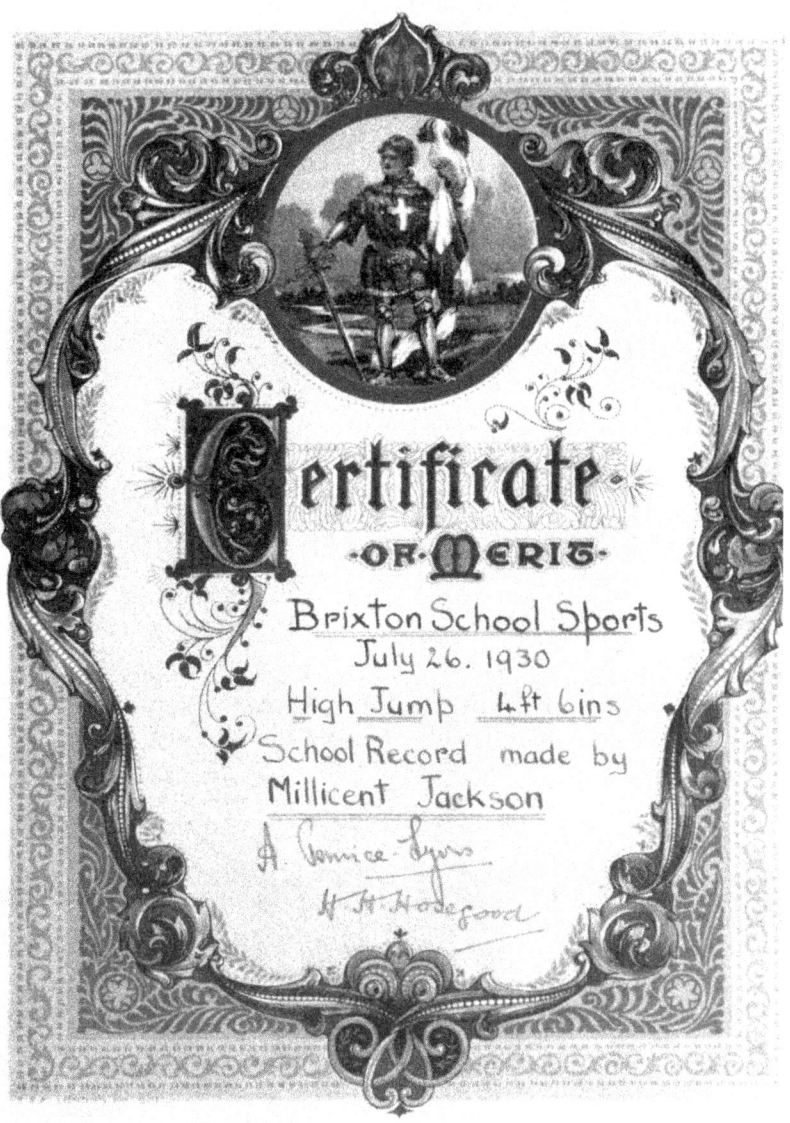

Brixton with Spriddlestone, Hareston Winstone & Coombe 4½ miles east from Plymouth, is a parish and pleasant village bounded on the south east by the estuary of the Yealm, in the Plympton St. Mary Union, Stonehouse county court district, Ermington and Plympton petty sessional division, Totnes archdeaconry, and Plympton hundred and rural deanery. The church is an ancient building in the Decorated style, and has a lofty tower and five bells. The living is a vicarage in the patronage of the dean and canons of Windsor, and is valued at £107. H. J. Eccles, Esq. is lord of the manor. Population of Brixton 1881, 686.

Post Office.—John Stone, postmaster. Letters are received through Plympton at 7.15 a.m. and despatched 5.30 p.m. on week-days. On Sundays they are received at 7.15 a.m., and despatched 9.40 a.m. The nearest money order office is at Yealmpton. Plympton is the nearest railway station.

Church.—Rev. Theophilus Jones, vicar.
National School.—Mrs Ann Cornish, mistress.
Rate Collector.—John Henry Northmore.

1882

Cockram Mrs Sarah, Rose villa
Collins-Splatt Henry, J.P. Brixton house
Eliott Thomas, Spriddlestone house
Jones Rev. Theophilus (vicar)
Lane Rev. Richard (vicar of Wembury), Brixton lodge.
Morshead Mrs Charlotte, Whifferden
Toop Jonathan
Moon John Edward, Cloudsleigh
Younge James Edward, Ellbridge house

Bastin Benjamin, farmer, Spriddlestone Barton
Blatchford William
Cane Benjamin, farmer, Torr hill
Cane Benjamin, wheelwright, &c.
Cane Joseph, farmer, Venn farm
Chaffe Richard, dairyman
Chaffe Richard, jun., *Foxhound inn*
Cockram Parnell, farmer, Wollaton
Cole John, farmer, Winstone
Coleman Samuel, blacksmith
Cornish Mrs Ann, schoolmistress
Eccles Henry Jennin, farmer, Hareston
Ford Richard, farmer, Butless
Hallett John, farmer, Sherford Barton
Lethbridge Christopher, farmer, Hareston
Lister William, bootmaker, &c.
Lashbrook John, miller, Cofflett mill
Mullis Joseph, farmer, Blackpool
Newman James, farmer, Spriddlestone
Northmore John Henry, butcher
Pursley William, farmer
Rowe Benjamin, farmer, Vale Home
Rowe Henry, farmer
Rowe John, farmer, Ford brook
Rowse Samuel, mason
Sparks William, farmer, South Bardon
Stone John, grocer and postmaster
Stooke James, farmer, Sherford Barton
Turpin Charles, Chittleburn farm
Wright Robert, bootmaker

BRIXTON is a parish and village on the road from Plymouth to Modbury, with a station at Brixton road, 1 mile from village, and 5 miles from Plymouth North road, 5 miles south-east from Plympton station on the South Devon section of the Great Western railway and 5 east from Plymouth; it is in the Tavistock division of the county, Plympton hundred, Ermington and Plympton petty sessional division, Plymouth county court district, in Plympton St. Mary union, and in Plympton rural deanery, archdeaconry of Plymouth and diocese of Exeter. The church of St. Mary, built in 1478, is an edifice of stone in the Perpendicular and earlier styles, consisting of chancel, nave, aisles, vestry, south porch and a lofty embattled western tower containing a clock and 5 bells, all cast by Abel Rudhall, of Gloucester, in 1737: the church was partially restored in 1887, at a cost of £2,500, and further restored in 1894 at a cost of about £2,000 and now affords 316 sittings. In November, 1899, a piece of ground was given for the enlargement of the churchyard by Hawrey Collinssplatt esq. and it was subsequently extended in 1919 so as to include a further piece of land presented by Miss Collinssplatt: the tower was restored in 1929 at a cost of £115. The register dates from the year 1658. The living is a perpetual curacy, net yearly value £350, with residence, in the gift of the Dean and Canons of Windsor, and held since 1924 by the Rev. Francis Rought Wilson. There is a United Methodist mission hall. The Brixton Institute was the gift of Miss Frances Collinssplatt. A charity of about £29 yearly, derived from parish lands, is equally divided between the poor and general church purposes. The Kennaway endowment, founded in 1874 and amounting to £1 2s. 6d. yearly, is equally divided between the poor and the schools. The Binnear charity produces £4 10s. yearly, which is distributed in coals to the aged poor. A family, taking its name from this place, was anciently resident here, as were also the Calmady, Copleston, Drake, Fortescue, Maynard and Pollexfen families; the Heles held the mansion in the 17th century, and in 1635 Eliz. Hele, of Wollaton, bequeathed it with her other estates to charitable uses. The land is divided among several owners. The soil is loamy; subsoil, limestone. The chief crops are wheat, barley and green crops. The area is 3,128 acres of land, 3 of tidal water and 94 of foreshore; rateable value, £7,877; the population in 1921 was 726 in the civil and 598 in the ecclesiastical parish.

Sexton, Peter Salter.

Post, M. O., T. & T. E. D. Office (letters should have Devon added).—Charles Goad, postmaster
Public Elementary School (mixed), for 140 children; Hugh Henry Hosegood, master
Railway Station, Brixton road, Albert H. Robertson, station master
Clerk to the Parish Council, Alfred Folley, Plympton St. Maurice

PRIVATE RESIDENTS.
(For T N's see general list of Private Residents at end of book.)
Anderson-Morshead Misses, Wiverton
Collinssplatt Mrs, Brixton lodge
Grattan Mrs, Rosemont
Marshall Capt. Frank J. Brixton ho
Miller A. W. H. The Way
Moon Mrs. Cloudesleigh
Penrice-Lyons Comdr. Algernon Edmund D.S.O. Ellbridge
Sergeant William George, Spriddlestone house (postal address, Plymstock)
Snow John, Wiverton Acre
Wilson Rev. Francis Rought (vicar), Vicarage

1926

COMMERCIAL.
Market thus † farm 150 acres or over.
†Atwell Jn. farmer, Spriddlestone
Boulace Jn. Fras. Fox Hound inn
Cane Benj. farmer, Torr Hill farm
Cane Jsph. farmer, Venn farm
†Chaffe Hy. J. farmer, Higher Hareston
Clark Edwin Albt. butcher. T N Yealmpton 35X3
Crocker Frank, dairyman, Elmsleigh
Elliott Mary (Mrs.), shopkpr
Gilley Charles, insurance agent
Goad Chas. shopkpr. & post office
Griss Geo. gardener to Lt.-Col. R. Bastard D.S.O. The Gardens
†Hallett Jn. Rew. farmer, Sherford barton
Harris Wm. gamekeeper to Lt.-Col. R. Bastard D.S.O. Winston
†Harvey Henry, farmer, Halwell
Haydon Alfred, farmer, Wappiewell
James Ernest Edwd. frmr. Ford Brook
James Harold Fredk. carpntr
Mann James, wheelwright
†Manning Chas. farmer, Gorlaven
†Manning Sydney, farmer, Wollaton
Newman James, farmer, Spriddlestone
†Norton Mrs. Jane Rowan Hendy, farmer, Veal holm
Ottley Jn. Hy. grocer
Radmore Ernest A. farmer, Spriddlestone
Rogers Henry, haulier
†Rowe Sarah Beatrice (Mrs.), farmer, South farm
Sergeant Wm. Geo. frmr. Spriddlestne
Smallridge Samuel, farmer
South Hams Brick Works (Western Counties Brick Co. Ltd. proprs)
†Symons Jn. Walt. farmer, East Sherford. T N Plympton 105Y
Turpin Bros. farmers, Chittleburne
Yealm Oyster Fishery Co. Ltd. (Jn. Kingcome, managing director)

Local Trade Directories

A very good source of names, dates, trades and professions can be obtained from these books in the Plymouth library. They were produced about every five years or more from the 1850s and ceased at the Second World War.

Methodist centenary

THE village of Brixton is to celebrate 100 years of Methodism next week with a special 'Country Flower Festival'.

The Methodist Church, on the corner of Steer Point Road, plays host to the festival on Friday, Saturday and Sunday (July 12-14), which will include displays made by members of the church. Each arrangement will depict a certain hymn.

The festival will be opened by Mrs. Evelyn Dickinson, wife of the minister, the Rev. Joseph Dickinson, at 10.30am next Friday, and stays open until 8pm. The opening times on Saturday are 10am to 8pm, and on Sunday from 10am to 5pm. Admission is 20p, programmes are available on the door, and refreshments will be served all day.

Methodism began in Brixton in the mid-1880's, when a Methodist Society was formed in the village. At that time, there was no headquarters, and the 'congregation' had to meet in each others' houses.

This situation was changed in the early 1900's due to the building of the Yealmpton railway line, which passed close to Brixton. An old tin hut, used in the building of the railway, was sold off to Brixton Methodists, who placed it on the corner of Steer Point Road and named it Brixton Methodist Church.

The hut remained there until 1958, when it was taken down to make way for the present building.

OPENING AND DEDICATION

of the new

BRIXTON METHODIST CHURCH

on Saturday, September 6th, 1958, at 3.30 p.m.

ADMIT BEARER

Please be in your place by 2.45 p.m. after which time the Stewards may be unable to reserve it for you

The Old and the New Side by Side
The main road was then much narrower as the old tin building stood right in front of the new Methodist Church opened in 1958. Note also the wartime air raid shelter.

The First Chapel Building
Originally used by the builders of the Yealmpton railway which opened in 1898, this quite large tin building was brought to this site and converted into a place of worship just after the turn of the century. It stood here until 1958.

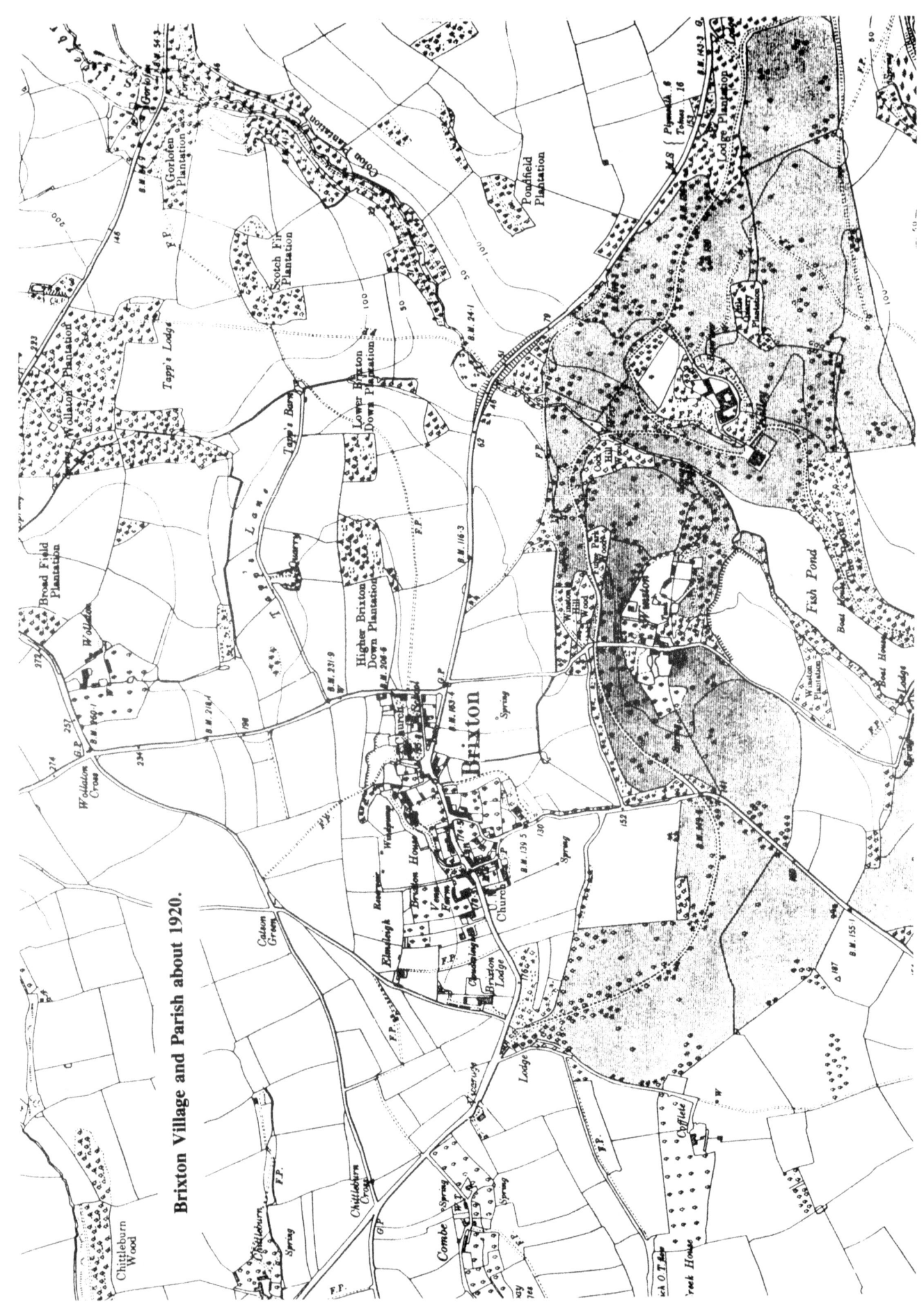

Arthur L. Clamp – the man behind the books

Arthur Leslie Clamp was a man of boundless energy with a passion for helping others, particularly through his love of history. A printer by trade, he started his career in a printing company before moving his family from Exeter to Plymouth to teach at the Plymouth College of Art and Design, where he eventually became the Head of the Printing Department.

Arthur with his five children.

A Devoted Family Man

Despite his love of teaching, Arthur prioritised his family, always making it home by 5:30pm for tea. He and his wife, Rosemary, raised five children: Susan, Angela, Elizabeth, David, and Steven. Arthur would often combine his love of family and history by taking his children on Sunday walks, encouraging them to appreciate historical monuments by taking photos or making crayon rubbings of gravestones for his books. The family home at 203 Elburton Road was a hub of activity, with a large garden, featuring a two-storey fort and a makeshift swimming pool.

A Lifelong Learner and Adventurer

Arthur's thirst for knowledge extended beyond history to a deep curiosity about the world. He was passionate about exploring different cultures, traditions, and cuisines, often taking advantage of his long summer holidays as a teacher to travel to places like India, Russia, South America, the middle east and the USA, sometimes bringing one of his children along. This adventurous spirit even influenced his home life, as seen by the short-lived family tradition of steam-cooking vegetables after a trip to Iceland.

History is a prominent feature of family days out

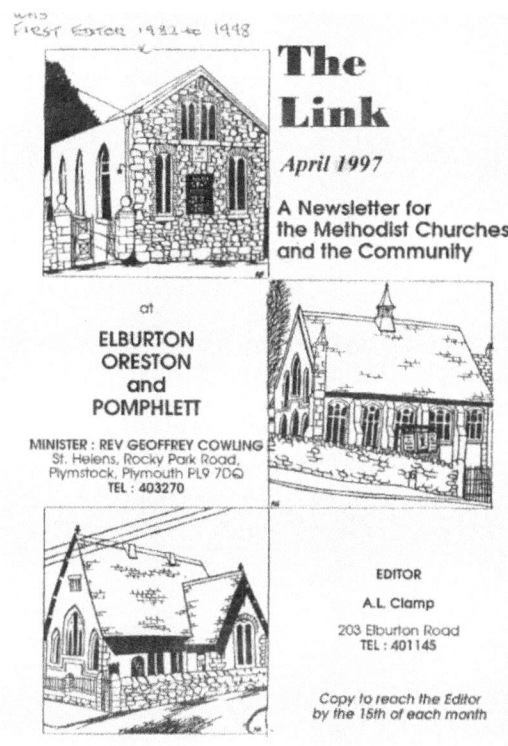

Community and Philanthropic Spirit

His commitment to serving others was evident in his long-standing involvement with the Elburton Methodist Church. He was the Sunday School Superintendent for over 15 years and served as the editor of the wider church's monthly newsletter, "The Link," for a similar duration. After Rosemary's very sad passing, Arthur later remarried and, following a chance encounter with a professor from India, established a connection with a missionary school in Chennai. Together with his new wife, Christine, he co-founded a "Sponsor a Child's Education" program that continues to this day.

*Pictured left – The cover of 'The Link' complete
with hand drawn sketches of each church by Angela
Below right – Arthur Clamp promoting his latest book
Below left – Arthur at home with his first wife, Rosemary
Below centre – Arthur on holiday with his second wife,
Christine*

A Legacy of Learning and Positivity

Arthur's greatest passion was history, which he brought to life through tireless research, documentation, and the many books he authored. He was driven by a need to "never be stuck in a rut," constantly seeking new experiences, meeting new people, and expanding his knowledge. With a positive attitude and a great sense of humour, he was always ready to help others, leaving a lasting impact on his family and community. His children, Susan, Angela, Elizabeth, David, and Steven, remember him with love and gratitude.

David Clamp, 2025

A Legacy of Local History

Below is the story of how Arthur L Clamp began writing books, in his own words, drafted shortly before he passed away in 2001. I have only made minor alterations to this text, correcting grammatical errors that he did not survive to correct himself. When I first discovered this text, I was shocked to see my name mentioned. It seems that, unbeknownst to me, I shared my first PC with him. I suspect he used it during the day when I was at school, although I do have one memory of sitting with him and showing him how it worked. It has been a pleasure to pick up where he left off and see his books republished and redistributed, and to know that I was part of the story, even back then. It was also fascinating to discover that his pricing structure matches the way I have tried to price the books, with a third going to local sellers and the rest covering printing costs with a little left over for my expenses.

I am his eldest grandson, and it is a privilege to curate his legacy, which we are calling 'The Clamp Collection'. The very last line of the text originally reads "The following pages list all the titles." Sadly, that page is missing and we have no record of all the books he published and knowing that some of those were researched by other authors makes the process of finding them even harder. I look forward to one day completing the collection and seeing them all available again. And maybe, one day, I'll even start writing my own to add to the series. For now, here is his story in his own words.

Steven Gibson, 2025

Writing and Publishing Booklets on Local Topics and Areas

I started this interest in either 1968 or 1969 when living in Woodford. I had by these dates established the Department of Printing and I think I must have been looking for something different to do. The first titles were of A5 size proofed from type set at Clarke, Doble and Brendon, Ltd., Plymouth printers, and then made up into pages and printed at Sawtell and Neilson, Ltd., Totnes.

Then began a slow process of getting them out to shops, etc. which proved to be more time consuming and difficult than actually researching, writing and getting the books into print. However, I persisted and opened a business account with Barclays Bank on the Broadway. I was advised to give it a title so I called it "Westway Publications". There came along another problem, one of storage of paper and finished books which was solved when the family moved to Elburton in 1970.

I changed the printer to Penwell, Ltd., Callington, Cornwall, as he was then just setting up himself and his prices seemed very reasonable. I did not get any of the printers to make up the complete books. I hand folded the flat printed sheets, stitched the books on a small manual table stitcher and trimmed them in a small hand turned guillotine which I bought from someone in Penzance for £40. It was brought up in a van.

The trouble and time going to and fro to Callington was too much so I transferred the printing to PDS Printers, Prince Rock, Plymouth, and I have been with them ever since. Now they are at Plympton which is easy to reach and they fold the flat sheets which was turning out to be a long chore which only saved a small part of the printing costs.

All my first titles were written by myself. I took the photographs and developed them in the loft of the house, the type was set by now on a computer situated in the house at Elburton from which I had collected photographic lengths of text to cut up and law down as pages.

At some point I decided that I would do my own film processing of lith film so I bought a large second hand process camera from Kingsbridge and learnt through trial and error to make line negatives of the text and halftone negatives of the illustrations which proved more difficult than I anticipated. The main problem was trying to keep the developer in the large dish at the correct temperature as any change would affect the developing time. I replaced this old camera with a brand new one bought from Croydon, Surrey, costing £900. This has turned out to be a great asset cutting out an expensive part of the printer's costs and one crucial aspect of the work which I could control.

By the middle 1970s there were many outlets I had contacted in Plymouth, up to Dartmoor, Exeter, around to Torbay, Totnes, Dartmouth and the South Hams. The market for local books was much greater than I had first thought and through getting to know many local people undertaking research themselves had the chance to help and make up books for other people who had in most instances, got together a collection of photographs with some text in a rather muddled way. Through my experience in print I was able to shape up their work and get it into print and in every case I had to pay the printer and let the person have the royalties. In the majority of titles produced in this manner this was another way of producing titles and it did give some profit to my work. However, I must say that in a few cases I lost out by either the other person getting the numbers wrong, not returning any monies from stock I delivered or they thought that more of their books should have been sold.

The print run was usually 1,000 copies and from time to time I have had reprints of 250 copies. It took about ten years to clear the first print run so I always had large stocks in the garage, workshop, etc. The numbers sold during the early years was about 7,000 copies a year increasing to around 9,000 copies and for the whole of the enterprise about 500,000 have been sold. The booklets have become part of the local scene and many people collect them, shops regularly order copies and I go around certain areas month by month restocking or replacing titles as necessary.

During the past year or so I have started setting the text on a Packard Bell PC, something which I should have done some years back. I share it with Steven Gibson, my grandson. There appears to be no end to the market for local books, but I could not earn a regular income because of the long time it takes to sell stock.

However, now exceeding 100 titles made up mainly of A4 twenty-four page booklets, some folded guides, with selling prices set with a third going to the shop which is the trade custom, the original idea has been quite successful and could go on for ever.

Apart from monetary benefits, however spasmodically these might be, I have learnt a lot myself, met many interesting people and have become part of the local scene with requests to give talks and to advise people about getting into print.

Arthur L Clamp, 2001

This newspaper article, published by the Evening Herald on 17th August 2001, forms a good record of his life. Just as he encourages us to learn more about local history, we encourage you to learn a little about him. For that reason, we have included these pages at the back of all the most recently republished books, in honour of his memory and recognition of his contribution to the community.